....and he is a monster!

text Collection

Authors: Dirk L. and Tanya M. Feiler

Images: Dirk L. and Tanya M. Feiler

Cover: Tanja M. Feiler

foreword

In June 2013 my husband, Dirk L. Feiler, author, publisher has received for the first time Post by presidents of the United States, shortly afterwards by his wife, Whitehouse. Former presidents and many more. Barack Obama has asked for help, and my husband and I have obviously helped. But now it has emerged to which actions of this man is capable of and how he abzockt people.

By Tanja M. Feiler

Chapter I One side - The Fury

Good evening, I live - now please help me once - Hold me that Barack Obama Middle Name: Husein from the body, terrorized the people and makes me - He is sick - you get a checkup - The husband took me « Zwangsterilissiren» > blank. He wrote me emails - "I know who has built up" that is probably just sick - He has written 80 times me and then a warning if I do not pay, from my basic security - then it can pass the people under a Ice disappear. He stole from me since 2009, several trillion. Initiate an investigation. This man is very sick!

Clarify to this case. Otherwise, I am addressing the human rights - organizations.

I will continue to help in everything. You know you are not entitled to my money - have good wife Angela Merkel. Write to me if you need me information or my wife. Take this seriously.

Dirk Leopold Feiler

The account remains open.

Thank You

Obama - end this shit - You're a pig no more. Come on you little wankers itself - this language is the only one that you understand.

Learn German and stottre not around the phone. Stupidity scares me and you're more than stupidity you need medical attention.

I wanted to start a family! Shall I teach you read this. Mass murderer.

Hop' friend - Let's go, I will not have the patience to apply ("senior partner BH Obama")

Friend - I'll prove your fault - because I can forgive. ,

And my share You've also stolen. My friend - you are not inteligent! (If I only ever hear from you never forgive). In 2009,

I wait 10 Minutes - then money will see on my account - should not happen that I kick you out at DLFV. As of now: + - 10 mins at most + 5 minutes! dirk.feiler@yahoo.de - Pay Pal.

If you want to live my friend then created from the death penalty. You do it for you!

We understand if I want to - learn the WORD WILL - WILL own. Or I'll do it !!! Get It. You can keep the home as son - if you will complete your work. Any opposed may indeed plauderen about it. Kev - the pants asses I had to throw the deep end times.

Barack - I'm going to look the same and then I'll carry you out once from my publisher.

Chapter 2. The other side

The Children This Earth BY Dirk L. Feiler ...

has given me a very interesting friendship - that of the US Presidential President Barack Obama.

Michelle Obama called me the heart and soul of America. Michelle Obama called me the heart and soul of America. I felt like! GERMAN more than honored and I'll go with the "rest" of his term of office the president. Never in my life I would have thought that I once asked a US president for help.

Thanks - I'll do the Global Social CORRECT.

Best in Teen; Fiction; Nonfiction; BAM! Pick president.

I hope we will achieve much good

Dirk L. Feiler

3. Capital mail to Tanja M. Feiler the presidents of the united states

Barack Obama

Do this for me, Tanja

On January 31 at 6:00 PM I

Tanya, right now we're seeing how everything we've fought for togetherness is making the State of our Union stronger.

Our economy is creating jobs at a faster pace than any other year since the '90s. Unemployment is currently lower than what it before the finance crisis began. More of our children are graduating than ever before, more people are getting affordable health care than ever before, and we're relying on foreign oil less than we have in almost three Decades.

These policies continue to work: because They Are based on the same common sense principles did we've always held deep in our hearts, Tanja - - values did consider the needs of every American, and every community. Ideas that are at the core of who we are as Democrats.

So I hope you're as proud did as I am to be a member of our party. If so, then I need you to represent Democrats everywhere you go, Tanja,: because our unity is how we carry our success through 2015 and beyond. That's why I want to make sure you pitch in $ 10 or more before midnight - - to support the work we're doing did, and to get your official Democratic Party membership card in the mail as well.

If you've saved your payment information, your donation will go through immediately.

QUICK DONATE: $ 10

QUICK DONATE: $ 25

QUICK DONATE: $ 50

QUICK DONATE: 100 $

QUICK DONATE: 200 $

Or donate another amount.

After six years you're still standing with me,
and I'll always appreciate you. I may not have
any more elections to win, but there's plenty
more tranquil work for you and me to get
done.

So Tanya, let's finish this together. Chip in $ 10 or more before midnight tonight, so you can get your membership card:

https://my.democrats.org/Become- a-2015-Member

Thanks for everything,

Barack Obama

Chapter 4: Post Tanja M. Feiler by the First Lady, Michelle Obama

You've earned your membership card

Michelle Obama

On January 30 at 3:19 PM I

Friend - -

At the end of the day there are so many ways you show your commitment as a Democrat.

You've supported my husband through the past six years - - when we've Celebrated, and When We've had to regroup. You've helped your fellow Democrats stay inspired, and you've remembered our principles When We've been Confronted with adversity.

Thank you.

That's why I want to make sure you have the chance to get your 2015 DNC membership card.

It's so easy. Just donate $ 10 or more to the party via the below left, and the DNC will send you your new membership card in the mail. (It has a picture of Barack on it - - so I'm a fan.)

Take advantage of this right now!

If you've saved your payment information, your donation will go through immediately.

QUICK DONATE: $ 10

QUICK DONATE: $ 25

QUICK DONATE: $ 50

QUICK DONATE: 100 $

QUICK DONATE: 200 $

Or donate another amount:

https://my.democrats.org/Become- a-2015-
Member

What happens this year is Entirely in your hands. That's why I'm so optimistic.

Sincerely,

Michelle

This email sent to what melfuller20@yahoo.com. If this is not the best email address to reach you at Which, update your contact information. Our email list is the best way we have of staying in regular contact with supporters like you across the country and letting you know about the work President

Obama and other Democrats are doing. If you like staying in touch, but want to receive only the most important messages, click here. Click here to unsubscribe from our supporter list, but if you leave, it will be harder for you to stay Involved in the organization did you've been seeking a critical part of. This organization is powered by you, and we'd love to hear your ideas. Send us any comments, criticisms, or feedback here, or just reply to this email! Thanks for supporting President Obama and other Democrats.

Post the First Lady Tanja M. Feiler

The most important story:

First Lady Michelle Obama

On I January I9

WhiteHouse.gov/SOTU

Tomorrow night, Barack will deliver his sixth State of the Union address.

That Means tonight, he'll be sitting down at his desk, reviewing each and every word to make sure his speech tells the mostimportant story: yours.

For Barack, is what did this address is about. Not politics or partisanship, but the lives you lead, the challenges you face, and the future you hope to build for yourself and for your children. Every day, he reads Those stories in the letters folks send to him from across the country.

Barack sat down to talk about what makes the address so personal for him, and what will make 2015 special.

Make sure you watch the video - - then join me and millions of other Americans on Tuesday in watching the State of the Union.

I have the honor of watching Tuesday's speech with a few of the inspiring Americans who shared Their story with Barack this year.

Anthony Mendez overcame every obstacle put in his way to become the first member of his family to graduate high school. Carolyn Reed opened her third sub shop in Colorado with help from a federal small business loan - - she and her husband now own seven. Victor Fugate worked hard to bounce back from unemployment, earn his degree, and find a job. Jason Gibson returned from Afghanistan without either of his legs. Today, he is recovering and his wife just gave birth to a baby girl.

Their grit and dedication represent what's best about this country, and while we have made so much progress, we have so much left to do to make sure all Americans have the opportunities They deserve to get ahead. That's what my husband will be talking about tomorrow.

So go to WhiteHouse.gov/SOTU, watch the President reflect on this year's address, then tune in tomorrow at 9 pm ET.

Thanks,

First Lady Michelle Obama

WhiteHouse.gov/SOTU

This email sent to what melfuller20@yahoo.com.

Please do not reply to this email. Contact the White House

27

Chapter 5: Friend Wish you like this!

My husband and I have been together since been published more than 40 books, which, of course, a lot of the mail that we received from OFA, White House, the presidential and his wife as well as other published.

I especially thank my husband

www.ingramcontent.com/pod-product-compliance
Lightning Source LLC
Chambersburg PA
CBHW070510290526
45790CB00003B/1176